SINGLE SKILLS

Subject Matter

Level **J**

*One Hundred Passages with Questions
for Developing Concentration and the
Skill of Understanding Subject Matter,
One of the Six Essential Categories
of Comprehension*

WALTER PAUK, PH.D.
*Director, Reading Research Center
Cornell University*

Jamestown Publishers
Providence, Rhode Island

SINGLE SKILLS SERIES
Subject Matter, Level J

Catalog No. SS71
Copyright ©1985 by
Jamestown Publishers, Inc.

Cover and Text Design by
Deborah Hulsey Christie.

Printed in the United States of America

3 4 5 6 7 AL 96 95 94 93 92
ISBN 0-89061-381-8

Prior knowledge is the key to understanding. For example, have you ever strolled through a museum and wondered why some people were fascinated by an object that looked quite ordinary to you? Prior knowledge gave them the edge. They knew the significance of what they were looking at, and by looking and understanding, they learned even more. And so it is with a page of print. Some people see only words, while others see fascinating meaning.

You, too, can see fascinating meaning in almost all factual writing if you have prior knowledge of these six components: subject matter, main ideas, supporting details, conclusions, clarifying devices, and vocabulary.

By knowing these structural components, it will be relatively easy and highly satisfying to scoop up the meaning of almost any factual passage.

In addition to teaching these all-important components, the *Single Skills Series* does one more essential thing: it teaches concentration. Wrinkled brows, compressed lips, contracted muscles, and held breath won't help anyone to concentrate while reading. Even saying, Concentrate! Concentrate! to oneself is self-defeating, for then you will be concentrating on concentration rather than on the printed word.

The slippery quality of concentration was readily recognized and insightfully expressed by William James:

> Trying to seize concentration is like seizing a spinning top to catch its motion, or trying to turn up the gas light quickly enough to see how the darkness looks.

Though William James identified and described the problem of concentration, he did not come up with a solution; but, we believe, we have. We devised the *anticipation technique,* which is a natural and uncomplicated method, and which is explained in the following pages.

Acknowledgements are now in order. First and uppermost, especial thanks and gratitude go to Robert Strauss. Bob, a writer of a novel, as well as many short stories, not only contributed passages to the series, but also, in a top supervisory capacity, did assist greatly in selecting, refining, and preparing multitudes of passages for final submission to the publisher. In short, he was the in-house editor-in-chief.

I am also eternally grateful to Ross James Quirie Owens, a writer, director, and cinematographer for his contribution of passages, sense of humor, advice, and friendship.

Finally and in high priority, I am indebted to all others who helped. Though not listed in this Preface, they are, nevertheless, inwardly listed and enscrolled forever in my memory.

w. p.
1985

Contents

| *To the Instructor*

The 100 passages in each book of the *Single Skills Series* are designed to help students develop skill in one of the six essential categories of comprehension: subject matter, main idea, supporting details, conclusions, clarifying devices, and vocabulary in context. Built into each reading passage is also a special device that helps students learn how to concentrate, thus comprehend better.

This particular book focuses on the skill of understanding subject matter. It contains 100 passages, each followed by one multiple-choice question that asks the students to select the answer choice that correctly expresses the subject matter of the passage.

Concentration. To help students develop the skill of concentration, a focusing device employing the *anticipation technique* is used. The last word of each passage is left out. To supply correctly that word, students must continually think while reading. As they read each sentence, they are to try to anticipate what is coming next. By constantly trying to anticipate what is ahead, the students are concentrating. If they have applied this technique throughout a passage, by the time they get to the last word of the last sentence, a word that makes sense in the context of the passage should come to mind. In fact, the exact word that the author intended often comes to mind.

If a word does not automatically come to mind, students have a second chance; immediately following each passage are three words. One is the correct final word for the passage. The other two are decoys. The students, scanning these word choices, should be able to choose immediately the correct word. If they cannot, then they know they were not concentrating carefully enough on what they were reading and that's a signal that they must try harder next time. Each time a student supplies the last word correctly, he or she is rewarded by the good feeling of having succeeded. To keep on getting this reward, students will make concentration a constant reading habit.

Skills Practice. The reading passages in this book are all factual, designed to interest a broad audience of mature readers, and written at a controlled reading level. The readability of each passage was computed by applying Dr. Edward Fry's *Formula for Estimating Readability*.

This book, and every book in the *Single Skills Series,* provides students with one of the most important elements in the learning of any skill: practice. By repeated practice with questions that are focused on a particular reading skill, students will develop an active, searching attitude that will carry over to the reading of other factual material. The skill question in each exercise will help students become aware of the subject matter of the material they are reading at the time they are actually seeing the words on the page. This type of thinking-while-reading helps readers achieve higher comprehension and better retention.

Introducing the Book. For practice to be truly beneficial, students must understand what they are practicing and why. The *To the Student* section of the book provides the basis for the practice. It explains thoroughly what subject matter is and how to approach the subject matter questions in this book. This section also highlights the importance of concentration and explains the concentration feature of the series. We suggest that you go through this section with your students, making sure that they understand how to do the exercises and how to correct their answers.

Worksheets, Answer Keys and Record Keeping. Students record their answers on reproducible worksheets. There are two different worksheets: one is designed for the main idea questions, each of which requires three answers, and the other is to be used for the remaining five comprehension categories. The answer keys for each grade level and individual student record-keeping sheets are provided for the teacher in convenient reproducible format.

If a student gets most of the comprehension questions wrong for several sessions in a row, have him or her reread the explanation of the skill and the sample exercise at the beginning of the book. Then have him or her reread some of the questions incorrectly answered and, with the correct answers in mind, reread the passages to discover why the correct answers are correct.

When a student answers most of the questions correctly for several sessions, you may want to advance him or her to the book at the next higher level.

CONCENTRATING

Do you know that you cannot concentrate on two ideas at the same time? Yes, the mind can bounce back and forth between two ideas. But, like a tennis ball, it can't be on both sides of the court at the same time.

If concentration is ever needed, it is when you read. What a waste of time to have your eyes glide over print while you are thinking about something else! The trick is to tie your attention to what you are doing.

Can you learn to keep your mind on what you are reading? Yes! This book is made to help you do just that. How? By using the *anticipation technique.*

Here's how the technique works: The last word of each passage in this book has been left out. Under the passage are three words. One of these is the correct last word. As you read a passage, you should pick up and hold information in your mind. Use each idea you read to try to guess what's coming next. Do this right up to the end of the last sentence. If you have been truly concentrating, a last word should come instantly to your mind, without your having to look at the three word choices.

After you have thought of a last word, look at the word choices. Quickly choose the one that correctly completes the passage. If you concentrated as you read, you will often find that the word you guessed would be the last word will be the right word choice. Write the last word in the space provided on your answer sheet.

If you cannot easily think of a last word that makes sense when you get to the end of a passage, you will know that you were not concentrating fully. This will tell you that you must try harder on the next passage.

Here's one more tip. To start concentrating, ask yourself, What is this passage about? You will find that by asking this question your mind will be drawn to the writer's words to find an answer.

SUBJECT MATTER

The subject of a passage is simply what it is about. It is the topic. In this book, you will be asked to find the subject matter of each passage you read.

When you have read the first few lines of a passage, ask yourself, What is this passage about? Asking this will make you concentrate on trying to find the subject matter of the passage. It will also help you to better understand and remember what you read. Try to find the subject matter of this passage:

> The people of ancient Egypt made mummies because they believed that the dead lived on in the next world. They wanted to preserve the bodies of the dead. It took seventy days to prepare a body. First the brain and organs were removed. The stomach was filled with linen pads. Then the body was placed in what we call soda ash until it dried out. It was then wrapped in many layers of linen strips and placed in a coffin. Some mummies have been preserved for thousands of years.

What is this passage about? If you read it carefully, you will agree that it is about mummies. All the details tell something about mummies. We learn how and why they were made and how long some have lasted.

For each passage in this book, you will be asked to find the subject matter. You will be given a question with four answer choices. Only one will correctly express the subject of the passage.

Below is a sample passage and question. Read the passage carefully. Begin by asking yourself, What is this passage about? When you get to the end, try to guess what the last word is. Then look at the three word choices that are given. Choose the one that correctly ends the passage. Next, answer the subject matter question. Explanations of the answer choices follow. These will help you understand how to think about this type of question.

> In A.D. 79, the city of Pompeii, in Italy, was a resort for rich Romans. The city had been built next to a dead volcano—Mount Vesuvius. But the volcano was not really dead. It was just sleeping. One day it erupted. It threw hot ash and stone on the city and filled the air with poisonous gas. Pompeii was destroyed, buried under many feet of cinder and ash. Today scientists have uncovered the ruins of Pompeii. They have found the remains of 2,000 people, the shapes of their bodies preserved like shells by hardened ash.

They have also restored many of the temples and palaces. Tourists can now walk through the ancient streets of this once great, but doomed, _____.

volcano   city   country

This passage is mainly about

(a) Mount Vesuvius.
(b) the ancient Romans.
(c) the city of Pompeii.
(d) volcanoes.

Did you concentrate as you read the passage? Then you know that the last word should be *city*. You have been told in the passage that Pompeii is a city.

In the subject matter question, *c* is the right answer. The very first sentence talks about Pompeii. All the other sentences relate to the city. They tell where it was built, how it was destroyed, and what scientists found when they uncovered it. Answer choice *a* is wrong because Mount Vesuvius is only mentioned as the cause of the ruin of Pompeii. Answer *b* is wrong because the Romans are only mentioned in one sentence. They often spent time in Pompeii. Answer *d* is wrong because only Mount Vesuvius is mentioned. The passage is not mainly about volcanoes.

As you answer the questions in this book, try to notice answer choices that tell only details from the passages. Look for what each passage is mainly about. And remember, the way to zero in on what a passage is about is to concentrate!

| *The Steps in a Nutshell*

Here is a quick review of the steps to follow in working your way through the practice passages in this book.

1. *Concentrate.* Ask yourself, What is this passage about? just before you begin reading.

2. *Read Attentively.* Pay close attention to each idea you read and try to anticipate what will be told next as you go along.

3. *Fill in the Last Word.* As soon as you get to the blank at the end of the last sentence, try to think of the word that should go there. Then choose one of the concentration words under the passage as the last word of the sentence. Write that word in the space provided on your answer sheet.

4. *Answer the Skill Question.* Read the question and all four answer choices. Mark your answer on your worksheet.

5. *Correct Your Answers.* Use the answer key to check your answers. Correct any incorrect answers according to the directions on your worksheet.

6. *Record Your Progress.* On your Individual Record Sheet, mark the numbers of the passages you completed, and put an x in the appropriate box for each concentration word or skill question you got wrong.

7. *Take Corrective Action.* Look again at the correct answer to each question you answered incorrectly. Then, with that answer in mind, read the passage once more, trying to find out why the correct answer is right.

1 | The New York subway system is the most extensive under-ground railway system in the world. The London subway system is actually longer than the New York system, but it has fewer miles of track that are underground. The London subways cover 252 miles of track, which carry six hundred trains made up of four thousand cars and transporting six hundred million passengers per year. The New York subway system has 230 miles of railroad tracks, of which 134 miles are underground. New York subways carry over two billion passengers yearly; that's about 4.5 million people using the subways every day. The New York subway system is also one of the few that has trains in operation twenty-four hours a _____ .

month   year   day

This passage is about

(a) why people choose to ride subways.
(b) the two biggest subway systems in the world.
(c) the advantages of using subways to get around cities.
(d) why the New York subway system is so well used.

2 | The Latin American country of Chile owes its independence from Spain to an army of sheep and cows, and to a very creative commander named Bernardo O'Higgins. In 1818 O'Higgins, a Chilean soldier and statesman, together with a small troop of rebels, fought an army of experienced Spanish soldiers. Although O'Higgins's rebels fought with courage, they were hopelessly outnumbered and came very close to defeat. When it looked like they were going to lose, O'Higgins devised an unusual plan of battle. He ordered his army to gather a herd of mules, cows and sheep. The rebels then stampeded the animals into the Spanish line. The Spanish army fled, giving the Chileans time to reorganize and win their war for _____ .

money   independence   Spain

The main subject of this passage is

(a) an unusual battle strategy.
(b) the history of Chile.
(c) the history of Spain.
(d) Chilean heroes.

14

3 | The United States has more domesticated cats than any other country. The cat population of the U.S. is close to forty million, with twenty-five million house pets and more than ten million strays. Various cat accessories, such as food, kitty litter, health care, and even comic books, are all part of a growing multi-million-dollar cat industry. Carefully-bred show cats sell for more than 250 dollars each. But animal shelters always have a large number of abandoned cats and kittens looking for good _____ .

cats   litters   homes

This passage is about

(a) the least popular pets in America.
(b) the popularity of cats in America.
(c) wild cats in America.
(d) pet cats around the world.

4 | Why do stories about sunken treasure always seem to involve Spanish galleons? Spanish galleons were sixteenth-century ships modeled after the English galleon, a swift battleship, and used by the Spaniards to bring valuables back from the Americas. The English galleon had both oars and sails, and was designed to be swift and maneuverable. But the Spanish version had a longer, higher poopdeck, which made it harder to steer. This high, swooping rear deck made the Spanish galleon look graceful, but it turned out to be a tragic flaw. Because the Spanish galleon was so hard to maneuver, it couldn't defend itself against pirates. Today, nearly two thousand Spanish galleons lie under the Atlantic Ocean, with their treasure still waiting to be recovered. The richest wreck found so far was the San Pedro, recovered in 1954 by two Bermudians. It contained thousands of gold bars, coins, pieces of jewelry, and the single most valuable object ever salvaged from the ocean—a thirty-thousand-dollar emerald-studded Bishop's

_____ .

cannon   gold   cross

This passage is about

(a) the Spanish economy.
(b) Spanish galleons.
(c) how England defeated the Spanish navy.
(d) finding treasure.

5 | From the eighteenth century to the early twentieth century, pigeon racing was considered a popular sport. During the 1920s, large amounts of money were bet on these races, but the practice was not always very profitable for gamblers. In one race that took place in July of 1928, from Havana, Cuba, to Washington, D.C., twenty-seven of the twenty-eight competing pigeons disappeared. The only bird to complete the grueling 1,175-mile journey was a pigeon named Eureka, and it was declared the winner by default. Pigeon racing became less popular with the construction of tracks for horse racing. Horse racing was a more reliable and profitable sport for _____ .

gamblers   pigeons   horses

This passage is about

(a) popular sports.
(b) gambling on animals.
(c) horse racing.
(d) pigeon racing.

6 | Vampire bats, which drink their victims' blood, are the source of many grisly legends. During the eighteenth century, European explorers in South and Central America discovered vampire bats. They returned with exaggerated stories, and the myths concerning these bats and vampires began to flourish. There are dozens of Eastern European tales linking the vampire bat with the myth of the human vampire. To separate the facts from the myths, the vampire bat is found in Central America, and it is known to attack people and other warm-blooded animals for their blood. Although the bite from a vampire bat often heals without complications, many bats carry rabies and other diseases that can infect their

_____ .

victims   bats   vampires

This passage is about

(a) explorers of the eighteenth century.
(b) facts about the vampire bat.
(c) Eastern European legends.
(d) diseases found in the tropics.

16

7 | Silk, which is one of the finest and most valuable fabrics in the world, is made from the cocoons of silkworm moths. The silkworm is an insect that is native to the Far East. Silkworm farmers in China and Japan raise tiny silkworm larvae, which are small caterpillars, by the millions. They feed them a steady diet of mulberry leaves, which are only available in the Far East. When a caterpillar stops eating, it is a sign that it is about to turn into a moth. It then attaches itself to a twig and begins to spin its cocoon. This cocoon is made of the silkworm's valuable silk thread. Because the caterpillar would damage its silk cocoon when it emerged as a full-grown moth, the cocoon is baked in an oven, killing the caterpillar but preserving the silk. The tiny silkworm caterpillar must die in order for people to have an elegant _____.

moth   caterpillar   fabric

In this passage the author discusses

(a) the birth of a silkworm.
(b) the production of silk.
(c) the fabric industry.
(d) the use of mulberry leaves.

8 | Baby blue whales gain weight faster, proportionally, than any other plant or animal. Following an eleven-month gestation period, the baby blue whale weighs an ample six thousand pounds at birth. By its first birthday the whale weighs an average of fifty-two thousand pounds. This rapid increase in weight can be attributed to two factors: first, the rich mother's milk on which the baby whale feeds, and second, the baby's rapid development of a thick layer of fat that protects it from the cold _____.

gestation   water   blubber

This passage deals mainly with

(a) how to weigh a baby blue whale.
(b) the rapid growth of the baby blue whale.
(c) how blue whales mate.
(d) the fastest animal in the world.

9 | An aristocrat, a slave, or a cow—if you believe in reincarnation, you might think that you will become one of these in your next life. Reincarnation, also known as transmigration of the soul, is the belief that the soul goes into the body of an animal or another human being after death. Belief in reincarnation forms a part of many religions, from those of ancient Greece and Egypt to modern Brahmanic Hinduism and Buddhism. For Buddhists, reincarnation serves to purify the soul. The soul passes from one body to another until it is completely pure. It then returns to the dwelling place of its god, which the Buddhists call *nirvana*, or eternal peace. Brahmanic Hindus believe that the soul eventually joins Brahman, the Universal Power. They also believe that a person's character in this life determines what he or she will be in the next life. For instance, if a person lives like an animal, he or she will return to Earth in the body of an _____.

animal   god   Hindu

This passage concerns itself with

(a) belief in reincarnation.
(b) a history of Buddhism.
(c) the use of religion in foreign countries.
(d) religions in ancient history.

10 | Milo, a Greek athlete in the late sixth century, was the greatest wrestler and all-round competitor of the early Olympics. Legend states that Milo carried a heifer (or an ox) through the stadium at Olympia and, after the Olympics, ate the entire animal by himself. According to sixth-century historians, Milo performed so many feats of strength that he easily won the public's admiration. He was so strong that he could lift a life-sized, bronze statue of himself. Also, while standing on an oiled disk, Milo would challenge competitors to attempt to push him off the _____.

disk   statue   Olympics

This passage is about

(a) Greek athletes.
(b) early Greek legends.
(c) Milo, an ancient Olympian.
(d) the Olympics of the sixth century.

11 | People of the ancient world had the technique for making ice cream, but they lacked the proper ingredients. As long ago as 1550, Romans used ice found in the mountains to cool their beverages. They also discovered that they could produce a frozen mixture by adding salt to the ice, and when honey or fruit was added to this mixture, the result was a type of dessert called an ice, which is still popular today. A thousand years later, Marco Polo brought the world closer to the discovery of ice cream when he returned from the Orient with a valuable recipe for a dish known as ice milk. It took several more centuries before cream was substituted for milk, and the world was treated to a new dessert called ice _____.

cream   milk   honey

This passage is about

(a) desserts from ancient times.
(b) the history of ice cream.
(c) the journeys of Marco Polo.
(d) ingredients used in desserts.

12 | Most people who've ever been anywhere near a piano know how to play "Chopsticks." A hundred years ago, many families owned pianos, but the only thing most people could play was this simple little tune. "Chopsticks" was written because many people insisted on having a musical instrument in their homes but didn't want to go through the labor of learning how to play it. Thus, most pianos simply sat in a corner, unused. Finally, someone came up with the idea of a one finger piano composition—"Chopsticks." Thousands of similar pieces were written during this period, and the world's pianos rang with those simple, bright little melodies. But of all the ones that were composed, only "Chopsticks" remains

_____.

fast   popular   loud

The subject of this passage is

(a) the invention of the piano.
(b) the history of "Chopsticks."
(c) the history of the piano.
(d) how to tune a piano.

13 | Many American movies that are popular in the United States are sent overseas. During the 1960s, a movie called *The Sound of Music* was released. It was a film that almost everyone in the United States enjoyed. Although it was longer than most films, it was filled with charming and memorable songs that became very popular. A movie manager in South Korea decided that *The Sound of Music* would please his patrons, but he felt that there was one problem with the film: it was too long. He decided to edit it and, believe it or not, he shortened the movie by cutting out all of the

_____.

films   words   songs

The subject of this passage is

(a) the making of *The Sound of Music.*
(b) popular songs from films.
(c) what happened to *The Sound of Music* when it went to Korea.
(d) the reason *The Sound of Music* is popular overseas.

14 | The steinkirk (STEEN-kuhrk), a special tie worn by Boy Scouts, was invented during a battle. In 1692, French soldiers were garrisoned in the Belgian town of Steenkerke when they were suddenly attacked by the British forces. Normally the French soldiers wore carefully tied pieces of cloth called cravats (kruh-VAHTS) around their necks. Because the British attack was unexpected, the French soldiers didn't have time to dress properly, and they quickly knotted their cravats about their necks. A new fashion was created by the successful French troops, and by the eighteenth century the steinkirk was a popular accessory of stylishly dressed men and women. Today, this once fashionable scarf is usually worn only as part of the uniform of a Boy _____.

Explorer   Scout   Belgium

This passage is about

(a) the history of the cravat.
(b) the uniform of a French soldier.
(c) the history of the steinkirk.
(d) the town of Steenkerke.

20

15 | Many male birds use a variety of mating dances or songs to attract mates, but the Australian bowerbirds rely on well-decorated structures to attract females. The male bowerbird constructs a bower (room) or a series of passages arched over with twigs and grasses. After the chamber is built, it is decorated with bright-colored objects, and often these bright decorations are laid on beds of green moss at the entrance to the bower. Many times a male bird will adorn the bower with objects that are all the same color. For example, in 1940 an ornithologist (or-nuh-THAHL-uh-juhst) discovered a bower made of blue bags, a blue railroad ticket, blue beads and a blue hair ribbon. The rooms built by the male birds are for courtship only, and the nests in which the female lays her eggs are not decorated at all. A bower is strictly ornamental, but the nest is a simple structure built in trees and used to raise the bowerbirds'

_____.

decoration   courtship   young

This passage is about the

(a) study of birds.
(b) mating rituals of Australian birds.
(c) mating ritual of the bowerbird.
(d) study of ornithology.

16 | In 1315, a French aristocrat named Enguerrand de Marigny was convicted of being a witch and put to death. De Marigny's son, Enguerrand de St. Cloud, believed that the courts had convicted his father wrongly. He tried to persuade the king to clear his father's name, but met with little success. So, de St. Cloud swore that he would wear a suit of armor until the monarch publicly pardoned his father. Seven years later, in 1322, the king finally agreed to pardon de Marigny, and de St. Cloud released himself from the prison of his _____.

father   armor   king

This passage is about

(a) witch burnings in the fourteenth century.
(b) the efforts one man made to clear his father's name.
(c) how kings decide to pardon criminals.
(d) the monarchy in fourteenth-century France.

17 | Plans are now being made for a flying oil tanker—a huge airplane, longer than a football field and with a wingspan of 160 yards, to be used to transport fuel. In one trip such a plane could carry up to two million pounds of cargo, including oil, liquefied gas or even water for drought-ridden areas. The advantages of air transportation would be faster delivery time and more flexibility in trading with other countries. The disadvantages include the amount of noise such a plane would make and the amount of fuel it would need to fly even a short distance. Also, planes are more likely to crash than supertankers, and one can imagine the explosion that would result from a plane crashing with one thousand tons of _____ .

> passengers   gas   footballs

The subject of this passage is

(a) an airplane used for fuel transport.
(b) the uses of air tankers.
(c) the amount of fuel used in airplanes.
(d) the future of airplanes in rapid transport.

18 | An Israeli doctor named Florella Magora has invented a device that uses electricity to induce sleep in people suffering from headaches, ulcers and even mental illness. The device has three wires. One attaches to the back of the head and the other two attach to the forehead. An electrical current runs through the wires and soothes the patient. The amount of electricity used is so small that it's impossible to be hurt by it, and the patient can operate the device on his or her own. Dr. Magora hopes that one day her invention will replace aspirin as a means of reducing the pain that keeps some insomniacs _____ .

> drugged   awake   asleep

This passage is concerned with

(a) why people suffer from insomnia.
(b) the use of aspirin in the future.
(c) an electric invention that helps people sleep.
(d) the cause of headaches.

19 | A famous English war song begins with the line "There'll be bluebirds over the White Cliffs of Dover." However, seeing bluebirds over Dover is very unlikely, since they are not found in England. There are two popular interpretations concerning the meaning of this line. Some say it refers to the blue uniforms of the Royal Air Force, whose airplanes were often seen flying over the cliffs during World War II. Others maintain that the line from the song refers to the symbolic bluebird of happiness, meaning that better and happier times for England were certain to come soon. Either interpretation offers a good explanation for the first line of the _____.

bluebird   song   war

The subject of this passage is

(a) the Royal Air Force.
(b) the different interpretations of an English World War II song.
(c) the natural habitat of the bluebird.
(d) the song of the English bluebird.

20 | Throughout the ages, many different types of weapons have been invented for wars. The American Civil War was no exception. Some strange proposals for new weapons included a rocket-powered torpedo, impenetrable body armor, and an armored hot air balloon. Both armies were considering a twin-barrelled cannon that shot balls connected by a chain. This cannon was supposed to mow down dozens of troops when fired at the enemy's front line. The Union was even offered an invention for walking on water that would have turned rivers into highways. With this invention, each soldier would have worn miniature canoes on his feet and sloshed along with the help of a tiny _____.

paddle   fortress   gun

The subject of this passage is

(a) ballooning during the Civil War.
(b) various causes of the Civil War.
(c) modern marine technology.
(d) strange ideas for weapons during the Civil War.

21 | The sort of reporting used in sensationalist newspapers is often called yellow journalism. That phrase comes from a rivalry between two newspapers in the late nineteenth century. William Randolph Hearst's *Journal*, during a circulation battle with Joseph Pulitzer's *World*, introduced a comic picture feature called "The Yellow Kid." This was one of the first comic strips to run daily. The editors of the *Journal* hoped that the comic would attract more readers to their paper. This kicked off a battle in which each newspaper tried to win more readers than the other by using big headlines, lavish illustrations and shocking stories. Because of this rivalry and the comic that started it, the use of gimmicks and sensational stories by newspapers became known as yellow _____.

paper   comics   journalism

This passage is mainly about

(a) the first daily comic strip.
(b) the origin of the term "yellow journalism."
(c) why newspapers use yellow journalism.
(d) the nineteenth-century rivalry between two papers.

22 | Some tribes in Africa have discovered some of the most deadly poisons known to humans. The Bushmen of South Africa developed a lethal poison from entrails of a kind of native caterpillar. Victims of this poison die in great pain and delirium. Hunting arrows are regularly covered with the poison, and sometimes they are dipped in it twice, if the intended game is a lion or other large animal. Some of the less exotic poisons are derived from scorpions, spiders and snakes. The Pygmies of central Africa have discovered a poison, extracted from red ants, that is so powerful it can kill a full-grown _____.

mouse   bird   elephant

The subject of this passage is

(a) Pygmy society.
(b) big-game hunting in Africa.
(c) deadly African poisons.
(d) the insects of the African jungle.

23 | The third set of molars, which are the last to erupt on either side of the upper and lower jaws of people, are called wisdom teeth. These teeth don't appear until late adolescence or early adulthood, which is why the name wisdom is used to differentiate these molars from earlier teeth. Third molars can be traced to early human evolution, when primitive people had larger skulls and a greater need for more teeth with which to grind food. Nowadays, most people must have their wisdom teeth removed because human skulls and jaws have become smaller over time. Because people's jaws are smaller than their primitive ancestors', and people don't require as much grinding power from their teeth, many anthropologists feel that wisdom teeth, through the process of evolution, will become _____.

extinct   larger   important

This passage is about

(a) the diet of primitive people.
(b) dentistry in ancient times.
(c) the evolution of wisdom teeth.
(d) dental diseases in primitive people.

24 | Johnny Carson and Dean Martin are stars, but they also have something else in common. They are members of the Turtle International Association. The club has a membership of about five million people. They hold an annual Turtle Queen Pageant and an International Turtle Creepstakes. A lifetime membership costs only one dollar. Members receive the club's bimonthly newspaper, *The Turtle Express*. The newspaper advertises a variety of items such as turtle pins, T-shirts and jackets. The club believes in a philosophy of Turtlism, which it sums up in its oath—"You can't get anywhere in life unless you stick your neck _____."

in   out   down

This passage is about

(a) an association that believes in Turtlism.
(b) an association that promotes celebrities.
(c) newspaper publication.
(d) lifetime memberships.

25 United States Secretary of State William H. Seward bought Alaska in 1867. He paid the Russians more than seven million dollars, which amounted to two cents per acre, for the land. Many people called Alaska *Seward's Folly* or *Seward's Icebox*, because they thought it was a useless frozen wasteland. However, Seward's purchase turned out to be a wise choice for the United States. Alaska is rich in fish, minerals, timber and potential water power. In fact, the value of the resources taken from Alaska has paid back its purchase price many times _____.

over   under   below

This passage is mainly about

(a) how Alaska got its name.
(b) mining industries in Alaska.
(c) Alaska's varied and rich resources.
(d) why the Alaskan purchase was a good idea.

26 In the summer of 1824, two alleged contractors named Lozier and DeVoe announced an ambitious project in New York City. They declared that they were going to uproot Manhattan Island, tow it out to sea, turn it around and bring it back. They reasoned that if the Battery were near the Bronx and Harlem were next to Brooklyn, Manhattan would never sink under the weight of large new buildings. Many New Yorkers supported this project. The two men signed up workers to do the excavations, and accepted contracts for supplies of food, equipment and giant anchors to keep Manhattan from being washed out to sea. They chartered enormous sailing ships to do the tugging. After two solid months of preparations, work was ready to begin. On a bright Monday morning, workers with their picks and shovels showed up, but Lozier and DeVoe didn't. They had managed to fool the entire _____.

city   sea   tow

The subject of this passage is

(a) the greatest bridge in history.
(b) two men who fooled the people of New York.
(c) a history of Manhattan Island.
(d) the revenge of the Manhattan Indians.

27 | In ancient Egypt, the crocodiles native to the Nile River were treated like royalty. To the ancient Egyptians, the crocodile was considered a sacred animal. The Egyptians believed that some animals, such as rams, falcons, and crocodiles, contained the spirits of certain gods. The crocodile was associated with the god of water. In cities where water was important to the quality of life, priests kept crocodiles in tanks on temple grounds. There they ornamented them with jewels and fed them the choicest foods. The city where the main crocodile temple stood was even named Crocodilopolis. When a crocodile died, its body was carefully embalmed and buried with great ceremony. It is not uncommon today for archaeologists to find crocodile mummies in some Egyptian ____.

rivers   tombs   streams

The subject of this passage is

(a) the use of crocodiles in Egyptian sacrifices.
(b) why all crocodiles were pharaohs of ancient Egypt.
(c) the Egyptians' treatment of crocodiles.
(d) how to tame a wild crocodile.

28 | The Olympic Games include a big marathon that isn't officially considered an event and that actually takes place before the Games begin. One of the symbols of the Olympics is a man running with a torch. Every four years, about 370 runners relay a lighted torch from the original site of the games in Olympia, Greece, to the current site in time for the start of the Games. The torch is called the Olympic flame, and the last runner uses the torch to light a larger, stationary torch called the Olympic fire during the opening ceremonies. The Olympic fire burns day and night for the duration of the _____.

Games   symbol   runners

The subject of this passage is

(a) a traditional pre-Olympic Games torch relay.
(b) training for the Olympic marathon.
(c) the Olympic torch-carrying competition.
(d) the history of the Olympic Games.

29 | Aspirin is believed to be the most widely-used drug in the world. Every year about twenty-two billion aspirin tablets are taken in the United States alone. That averages out to about one hundred tablets for every adult and child in the country. Of all the people taking aspirin, very few know how aspirin originated. This pain reliever was first used when the ancient Egyptians and Greeks discovered that chewing on leaves of the willow tree could relieve headaches and other body pain. It wasn't until the 1800s that the pain-killing substance, salicylate, was isolated. But taken in pure form, salicylate upset the stomach. A German chemist named Felix Hoffman developed a modified version called acetylsalicylic acid—modern aspirin. However, it was not until 1915 that aspirin was available in its present solid _____.

tree   liquid   form

This passage is about

(a) the life of Felix Hoffman.
(b) cultivating willow trees.
(c) the history of aspirin.
(d) old Egyptian remedies.

30 | The graham cracker was named after a minister. Sylvester Graham, who was born in West Suffield, Connecticut, in 1794, was interested in nutrition as well as religion. Graham soon discovered that he helped people more with his lectures on health and diet than with religious sermons. He supported the practice of eating mostly vegetables, beans and grains to keep the body healthy and pure. He also advocated the use of coarsely ground, unsifted flour, which quickly became associated with him. Graham crackers are made from this coarsely ground _____.

sugar   flour   vegetable

This passage is mostly about

(a) the original recipe for graham crackers.
(b) why graham crackers are healthy things to eat.
(c) the origin of graham crackers.
(d) why Sylvester Graham became interested in nutrition.

31 | The Sunday *New York Times* of October 17, 1965, was the largest newspaper edition ever printed. It had fifteen separate sections, 946 pages, weighed seven and a half pounds, and sold for fifty cents per copy. This single edition used up well over ten million pounds of paper in printing. The largest sheets of paper ever used for a newspaper were used in an 1859 Fourth of July celebration issue of another newspaper. George Roberts printed *The Constellation* in New York City on sheets that measured 51 inches by 35 inches. This paper size was only used for that one special _____.

television   radio   edition

This passage is about

(a) record-breaking news stories.
(b) a history of newspaper publishing.
(c) the largest newspapers on record.
(d) historically accurate newspaper reporting.

32 | Nervous people often say that they're feeling jumpy. But a nervous horse doesn't make a very good jumper. The horses that jump in shows and steeple-chases must be well-disciplined and calm. The high jump record for horses was set in 1949 by a horse named Huasó. Ridden by Captain A. L. Morales, Huasó leapt an amazing eight feet one and three-quarters inches into the air. Proving that horses can jump great distances as well as heights, Amado Mio bounded over more than twenty-seven feet of water in Barcelona, Spain, in 1951. Some people claim that a horse named Heatherbloom has broken both these records. They say that Heatherbloom has jumped eight feet three inches high and a distance of thirty-seven feet. However, neither of these records has been _____.

broken   set   proven

This passage is concerned with

(a) ways of proving world records.
(b) how horses react when they're nervous.
(c) world jumping records for horses.
(d) an amazing horse named Heatherbloom.

33 | One American vice president served his term on foreign soil. When Franklin Pierce was elected president in 1852, his vice president was William R. King. After the election, King fell ill with tuberculosis and went to Cuba to try to recuperate. He was too sick to return to Washington, D.C. in time for inauguration day, so Congress passed a special act allowing him to be sworn into office on foreign soil. King's health did not improve in Cuba, and he finally returned to Alabama, where he _____.

returned   died   voted

This passage is about

(a) Franklin Pierce's rise to power.
(b) a vice president who served in a foreign country.
(c) American-Cuban relations during Pierce's term.
(d) the constitutional powers of the vice president.

34 | The ancient artworks and architecture of both Egypt and Greece have taught scholars much about those ancient civilizations. Though Britain is not known as a great ancient center of civilization, it does have a monument that proves that a pre-Christian civilization lived there. But no one knows what the people who built the monument were like. Those ancient Britons left behind on the English countryside nothing but a circle of huge stones that we now call Stonehenge. According to English physicist Gerald Hawkins, the people who built Stonehenge knew both engineering and astronomy. The huge blocks of stone were somehow moved from Wales, three hundred miles away. The circle and the markers inside it cast shadows that indicate the position of the Earth, Sun and Moon. Stonehenge could predict the change of the seasons, the tides, and even eclipses. It may also have served as an altar to a sun god. Nothing else is known about those ancient people, except that they built Stonehenge more than four thousand years _____.

later   sooner   ago

This passage deals with

(a) how the pyramids were built.
(b) British society in 2000 B.C.
(c) how to tell time by the sun.
(d) an ancient British monument.

35 | Francis Gary Powers was a United States spy who was captured in the Soviet Union in 1960. Powers, a reconnaissance airplane pilot, was shot down over the Soviet Union just before a peace conference was scheduled to take place between the two super-powers. President Eisenhower admitted that Powers was a spy, and the pilot was sentenced to ten years in a Soviet prison. Fortunately for Powers, a Soviet spy was discovered in the U.S. the next year, and the two prisoners were exchanged. Powers did not stay in prison for _____ .

spies   long   months

This passage is about

(a) the U.S.-Soviet peace summit of 1960.
(b) the political power of President Eisenhower.
(c) an American spy who was caught and later freed.
(d) the U.S. and Soviet spy network.

36 | There are two main kinds of skiing—Alpine and Nordic. They are so different that only a few skiers can truly master both. In fact, only one skier in history has ever won Olympic medals in both styles. Nordic skiing, also called classic skiing, has been a competitive sport since 1866, when the first championships were held in Norway. Alpine skiing, commonly known as downhill or slalom, also dates back to the middle of the nineteenth century, in Austria. The two types of skiing are different because they developed under different ski conditions. Nordic skiing, which developed in the wooded hills of Scandinavia, includes cross-country skiing and ski-jumping. Alpine skiing, which developed in the European Alps, involves high-speed runs down steep mountainsides. Both styles are included in the Olympics and have their own separate world championships. No skier has won titles at both world championships, but at the 1936 Olympics, Birger Rudd of Norway won gold medals in both ski-jumping and the Alpine _____ .

downhill   motocross   mountains

This passage explains

(a) the differences between Alpine and Nordic Skiing.
(b) how to ski without getting injured.
(c) the difficulty of Olympic competition.
(d) how to find good places to ski.

37 | A new product has been invented that could make the world a little quieter: it's a noise-absorbing material called NEXDAMP. A steel and plastic laminate that comes in thin sheets, it absorbs noise and vibrations, and then transforms the absorbed energy into a small amount of heat. NEXDAMP can be applied to any flat surface, so its use is not limited to walls. Office equipment, cars, airplanes, and appliances can all be made quieter with it. An added plus to this noise-muffling material is that it is _____.

steel   laminate   inexpensive

This passage is about

(a) noise pollution in large cities.
(b) a new means of heating homes.
(c) a material that cuts down on noise.
(d) a new kind of insulation.

38 | Records have been established for just about any feat you can think of. Many involve traditional sports, but there are also a great number that are unorthodox, to put it mildly. Many hopeful record-breakers have gone underwater to make their claim to fame. Perhaps the most impressive record-breaking water feat was an underwater swim of the English Channel. It was performed by an American named Fred Baldasare in 1962. It took Baldasare eighteen hours and one minute to swim a forty-two-mile route from France to England. Of course, he did use scuba equipment. A more romantic record was set by Toshiaki Shirai and Yukiko Nagata of Tokyo, Japan, on April 2, 1980. They engaged in a two-minute, eighteen-second-long underwater kiss. Then there was the musically inclined Mark Gottlieb who played Handel's "Water Music" underwater on a violin in March 1975. He said that his biggest difficulty was trying to play individual notes quickly. No doubt Handel would have been surprised to hear that his music had ended up _____.

underwater   played   swimming

This passage is about

(a) how to break records.
(b) some unusual aquatic world's records.
(c) some scuba diving safety tips.
(d) some people who don't like the water.

39 | Modern orchestral music often requires the use of unusual instruments. John Cage's symphony *First Construction in Metal* is a good example. His score calls for twelve oxen bells, eight cow bells, five sound-effect thunder sheets, four Turkish cymbals, four Chinese cymbals, three Japanese temple gongs, tubular gongs, sleigh bells, a tom-tom, four percussion brake drums, and four blacksmith's anvils. Each of these instruments produces a different sound, so the combined effect includes most of the sounds that can be produced by _____.

wood   stone   metal

This passage is about

(a) music in the twentieth century.
(b) metal orchestral instruments.
(c) the unusual instruments in one of Cage's symphonies.
(d) the modern composer John Cage.

40 | A woman six months pregnant died of a brain seizure. Her doctor, William P. Dillon, knew that if the fetus were removed from the mother's body so prematurely it would have little chance of surviving in an incubator. Dillon decided to keep the mother's bodily functions running with sophisticated life-support equipment, even though her brain was clinically dead. Dillon hoped the mother's body would continue to nourish the baby until it grew enough to survive on its own. He was able to sustain the mother's vital signs for another six days, which turned out to be enough to insure the baby's survival. The fetus was removed by Caesarean section, and continued to develop normally. Although Dillon's attempt to keep the baby alive was successful, some other doctors have questioned the morality of using the dead mother as a kind of natural _____.

doctor   operation   incubator

This passage is about

(a) an unusual use of life-support technology.
(b) saving pregnant women.
(c) when to resort to Caesarean section.
(d) an improved way of incubating premature babies.

41 | It's usually safe to assume that something that is well built will last a long time, but it's never a good idea to stake your life on it. That's what King Christian IV of Denmark found out when he made what he thought was a safe declaration—that his reign would last as long as the tower of Saint Catherine's Church. The king made that pompous statement when he presided over the tower's dedication ceremony in the early seventeenth century. On February 28, 1648, the tower was leveled by a violent storm; King Christian died the same _____.

night   way   century

This passage is about

(a) seventeenth-century architecture.
(b) a remarkable coincidence.
(c) the reign of King Christian IV.
(d) unusual towers of the past.

42 | The corset has been modified over the years to keep up with the changing concepts of the ideal womanly figure. Actually, the corset is an ancient garment and was worn by both sexes as long ago as the Minoan Bronze Age (3000 B.C. to 1100 B.C.). From the 1550s to the 1660s, corsets were used to flatten the bosom. After the 1660s the hourglass shape became popular and corsets became shorter to accommodate the new "ideal figure." They supported the bosom, tightened the waist and flaired the hips. Throughout the 1800s corsets reinforced with whalebone and metal changed as the shapes of dresses changed. Although there was much publicity against the use of corsets, mainly for health reasons (corsets crushed internal organs and often broke ribs), they remained popular until the 1920s. During that era the new political and social freedoms experienced by women were also reflected in their clothing. Designs with straight, unwaisted lines finally freed women from the restriction of _____.

corsets   health   garments

This passage is about

(a) the women's movement.
(b) the Minoan Bronze Age.
(c) political freedom.
(d) the history of the corset.

43 | The northern coast of Colombia is a natural salt field. The ocean washes salt water onto the shallow beaches, and the water evaporates, leaving the salt behind. The Guajira Indians of Colombia harvest the salt once a year. Thousands of Indians go to gather the tons of salt that collected for ten months as the tropical sun evaporated the ocean water. Entire families work together to gather and bundle the salt into one-hundred-pound sacks and lug them to the salt merchants' trucks. The merchants pay the families ten dollars for one hundred sacks of _____.

water   ocean   salt

This passage is about

(a) farming in South America.
(b) the tropical seacoast of Colombia.
(c) salt manufacturers in South America.
(d) salt harvesting on the northern coast of Colombia.

44 | Chivalry can be nice, but it can also be taken too far. In Europe in the Middle Ages, chivalry was the code of behavior for the ideal knight. Knights were supposed to be exceedingly polite and honorable, especially toward women. Today, the word *chivalry* refers especially to overly polite behavior toward women. A man named Rodrigo Ponce de Leon once carried chivalry to an extreme. He was a fifteenth-century Spaniard renowned for his feats of bravery and kindness. One day, a lady named Ana de Mendosa dropped one of her gloves into a lion pit. As the story goes, Ponce de Leon leaped into the pit to retrieve the glove, although everyone there was sure he would be hideously mauled. But the gallant Spaniard, it is said, simply shooed the lions away, picked up the glove, and climbed out of the pit unharmed. Ponce de Leon was looked upon as a hero at the time, but today it seems strange to think that a man would risk his life for the sake of _____.

chivalry   attention   lions

This passage tells the legend of

(a) the way men earned knighthood.
(b) knighthood in the Middle Ages.
(c) the chivalry of Rodrigo Ponce de Leon.
(d) unusual Spanish customs.

45 | The most intricate carpet in the world doesn't fly, but it is still amazing. The carpet was completed in 1540 in Ardebil, Persia, and it measures 34½ feet by 17½ feet. The intricately-designed, colorful carpet is made up of 29 million knotted pieces of yarn, or more than 340 knots per square inch of carpet, and each knot was tied by hand. The carpet hung on the wall of the Mosque of Ardebil for more than three hundred years before it was moved to the Victoria and Albert Museum in England in 1893. It remains a testament to what can be achieved by talented and determined _____.

museums   designers   artisans

This passage is about

(a) the world's only flying carpet.
(b) tapestries in the Middle East.
(c) the most intricate carpet in the world.
(d) the Mosque of Ardebil in Egypt.

46 | The crew of the U.S.S. *Trout*, a submarine in World War II, would undoubtedly testify that gold and silver are worth little more than rocks in some situations. The submarine was assigned to ferry medical supplies to an American land force that was surrounded by enemy forces in the Philippines. All torpedoes and other heavy equipment were left behind on the voyage to cut down on weight and to make space for the cargo. The *Trout* reached its destination, but after delivering its cargo, the submarine didn't have enough weight to make a dive. The captain of the submarine asked the commander of the American forces for some gravel and rocks to use as ballast. The American commander said that his troops needed all such available materials for fortifications, but that the submarine was welcome to use two tons of gold and silver that was lying, useless, in a nearby bank. The precious metals did the job, and the *Trout* slipped out of the Philippines without being _____.

seen   banked   wet

This passage is about

(a) gold mining in the Philippines.
(b) a submarine that once used gold and silver as ballast.
(c) the sinking of the U.S.S. *Trout*.
(d) the causes of World War II.

47 | Henry Louis "Lou" Gehrig was one of the greatest American baseball players of all time. He played 2,130 consecutive games in fourteen seasons with the New York Yankees, and he compiled a life-long batting average of .340. He played with the famous Babe Ruth, and together they helped make the Yankees a team of legendary greatness. Many people remember Gehrig for the disease that forced him to stop playing baseball. It was a form of sclerosis that is now called "Lou Gehrig's Disease." He played his last season with the Yankees in 1939, and died only two years later, in _____ .

1941   1937   1939

This passage is about

(a) the great baseball player Lou Gehrig.
(b) the New York Yankees baseball team.
(c) the effects of sclerosis.
(d) the famous baseball player Babe Ruth.

48 | When someone has the same job for ninety-four years, you would think he'd get pretty good at it. Not so with Egyptian Emperor Pepi II, according to most historians. Pepi II had the longest rule of any monarch in history, and while he certainly did a good job of guarding himself against assassins or revolutionaries, he didn't do a very good job of running the country. Part of the reason was that Pepi II was only six years old when he ascended to the throne in 2500 B.C., and he never quite got over the fact that all his relatives had died. As an adult monarch, he was obsessed with the elaborate Egyptian funeral rites, and he spent much of his country's riches on building pyramids and filling them with treasures. The result was that Pepi II, obsessed with death, didn't serve the living kingdom well. Another reason that Pepi II wasn't a good ruler was that since his reign was so long he spent many years of it in _____ .

sorrow   tombs   senility

The subject of this passage is

(a) politics in ancient Egypt.
(b) the longest reign in history.
(c) Egyptian mummification practices.
(d) the building of the Egyptian pyramids.

49 | Charles Lindbergh, the first man to fly solo across the Atlantic Ocean, was more than an expert pilot. He also helped to develop an artificial heart. He researched and wrote a book about human physiology with French physician Alexis Carrel. Then he used his money and mechanical knowledge to help build a mechanical pumping device to aid the hearts of heart attack victims. The pump, a type of artificial heart, was a large machine that sat at the patient's bedside. Although he was mainly a pilot, Lindbergh used his mechanical knowledge for more than just _____ .

hearts   pumps   airplanes

This passage is about

(a) a description of Charles Lindbergh's historic flight.
(b) in-flight medicine in the days of Charles Lindbergh.
(c) Charles Lindbergh's work on a mechanical heart.
(d) the world's first heart transplant.

50 | Common mistakes that are usually no big deal can seem great when they are made on an important occasion. Queen Victoria's coronation in 1838 was certainly an important occasion, for it marked the beginning of one of the greatest periods in English history. But the ceremony became a near comedy of errors. First, the official ring, which was supposed to have been tailored to fit the queen's finger, was too small. The Lord of Rolle proved worthy of his name by tripping and rolling down the carpet while paying homage to the queen. Finally the service was over, and the queen was ushered out. The ten thousand guests started to leave, but they were soon milling about in confusion as the queen was brought back in. Part of the elaborate ceremony had been forgotten. After the ceremony was *really* over, Victoria returned to Buckingham Palace to perform her first act as queen—bathing her _____ .

ceremony   dog   carpet

This passage is about

(a) the end of Queen Victoria's reign.
(b) the Lord of Rolle.
(c) ways to avoid mistakes.
(d) the problems of Queen Victoria's coronation.

51 | No president before or since Franklin D. Roosevelt has held office for more than two terms. Roosevelt served four terms, and after his death during his last term in office, a law restricting the number of terms a president could serve was passed. This was done because many people feared that an unscrupulous president would take advantage of a lengthy term to permanently install himself in office. Roosevelt denied charges that he was trying to set up a dictatorship, and he rebuked supporters who suggested that he do so. Today's laws prevent a U.S. president from being elected more than two _____.

dictators   times   years

This passage is about

(a) the limit on the number of terms a U.S. president may serve.
(b) Franklin D. Roosevelt's administration.
(c) changes in the American electoral process.
(d) unscrupulous American politicians.

52 | John Brown was a United States abolitionist whose attempt to free the slaves in the country cost a number of lives and helped bring on the Civil War. Brown hated slavery from the time he was a youth, and he devoted his life to fighting it. He helped many slaves escape to Canada, and he fought to keep Kansas from becoming a slave state. In 1859 he and eighteen followers raided the U.S. Arsenal in Harper's Ferry, Virginia, planning to capture weapons to help lead a slave rebellion. They succeeded in capturing the arsenal, killing many people in the process, but then they became trapped in the town with no escape route. Brown and his surviving followers were caught, and Brown was put on trial for treason. He was convicted and hanged. Though he was a criminal, he was glorified for his deed by abolitionists throughout the country and by Union soldiers fighting in the Civil _____.

army   rebellion   War

This passage is about

(a) Harper's Ferry.
(b) the Civil War.
(c) John Brown.
(d) the U.S. Arsenal.

53 | In the late eighteenth century, most of the area that now makes up the five boroughs of New York City was still undeveloped marshland. Only Manhattan was widely settled. Brooklyn, Queens, the Bronx, and Richmond (Staten Island) were almost wilderness. Many battles of the American Revolution were fought in those undeveloped areas. Brooklyn was the site of an engagement between eight thousand American troops and a large contingent of British soldiers. The English planned to drive the Americans into the barrens of Long Island, but instead they themselves were forced to _____.

retreat   fight   win

This passage is about

(a) the level of development of New York City in the eighteenth century.
(b) the people inhabiting Manhattan in the late 1700s.
(c) New York's part in the American Revolution.
(d) famous battles of the American Revolution.

54 | Laminated safety glass is a "sandwich" made by combining alternate layers of plastic material and flat glass; if the glass breaks, the plastic holds it together, keeping it from shattering. Like many important inventions, safety glass was based on a discovery that was made by accident. A French chemist named Edward Benedictus knocked a beaker off his lab table one day, and it bounced when it hit the floor. He was surprised that the beaker had not broken, so he examined it more closely. He noticed that the beaker was coated on the inside with a thick celluloid material, a kind of plastic, that had dried on the glass. The plastic had prevented the beaker from shattering. Benedictus foresaw great potential for glass that would not break, and he worked for several years to refine his invention. He eventually developed the world's first laminated safety _____.

glass   plastic   celluloid

This passage is about

(a) French scientists.
(b) how to laminate safety glass.
(c) how to get rid of celluloid.
(d) the invention of laminated safety glass.

55 | When they form over the Atlantic Ocean, they're called hurricanes; over the South Pacific Ocean, typhoons. Over the Indian Ocean, huge, spinning tropical storms are called cyclones, and they may be the most destructive of all. A typical cyclone has three dangerous elements: heavy rains that can dump a foot of water on an area in one day, winds that gust up to one hundred miles an hour, and sea surges caused by the violent winds. Those three factors can do great damage to low-lying coasts, such as the one near Calcutta, India. In 1937 a cyclone there killed three hundred thousand people, and in 1970 a cyclone that hit the Bangladesh region took as many as five hundred thousand _____ .

lives   miles   storms

This passage is about

(a) Bangladesh.
(b) Indian storms.
(c) typhoons.
(d) cyclones.

56 | "Call the shark to the witness stand, Your Honor." Well, it didn't happen quite that way, but in 1799 a shark was found to have possession of evidence needed by a British court of law. The British court in Jamaica had charged Captain James Briggs of the U.S. ship *Nancy* with trading with enemies of the United Kingdom. Though the British were sure that Briggs was lying when he claimed to be on a legitimate coffee-buying mission, they didn't have enough evidence to convict him. Finally, a British navy lieutenant arrived with fresh evidence for the prosecution. He had incriminating documents from the *Nancy* that he had found inside the stomach of a shark he'd just caught. Apparently, Briggs had attempted to get rid of the papers by throwing them overboard, and the shark had swallowed them. So the British court convicted Briggs and seized his ship on evidence obtained from a _____ .

fish   criminal   lieutenant

This passage tells of

(a) the role a shark played in convicting a person of a crime.
(b) the shark-infested waters around Jamaica.
(c) British trade problems in Jamaica.
(d) the British legal system in the 1700s.

57 | The first American woman to earn a pilot's license was Mrs. Harriet Quimby of New York. She took her first flight lesson at Moisant Aviation School in Hempstead Plains, Long Island, on May 10, 1911. She qualified for her pilot's license by passing the required tests of the Aero Club of America. New pilots did not have to have much practice in flying at that time. Mrs. Quimby took thirty-three lessons, each lesson lasting from two to five minutes. That was the average length of a lesson in all the leading schools of aviation. Unfortunately, Mrs. Quimby's flying career was cut short; she was killed in an airplane accident a little more than a year after she had begun to _____.

fly   learn   land

This passage is about

(a) the invention of the airplane.
(b) the first licensed woman pilot.
(c) the early history of aviation.
(d) famous airplane accidents.

58 | Two hundred million years ago, the continents as we know them didn't exist. In 1912, the theory of continental drift, based on observation, was proposed. Scientists discovered that the coastlines of all the continents fit together much like the pieces of a jigsaw puzzle. Before the continents drifted to their present positions, they may have fit together into one large land mass. Many experts now agree that 200 million years ago the large continent split into several pieces, and that the pieces have been drifting ever since. The continents are still changing their positions on the earth's surface. North and South America are drifting away from Europe and Africa at about one inch per year. Recently, scientists have found evidence to support their theory. Coal has been found near the North and South poles. That means that at one time the poles were warm enough for plants to _____.

grow   drift   split

The subject of this passage is

(a) coal mining at the poles.
(b) the theory of the poles.
(c) jigsaw puzzles.
(d) the theory of continental drift.

59 | Carl Magee was the man who developed the first parking meter, allowing cities to charge for on-street automobile parking. At first, the city fathers in Magee's hometown, Oklahoma City, were doubtful that the meters would work. But the thought of collecting more money for the city convinced them to give the idea a try. So in 1935, Oklahoma City installed the world's first parking meters. Although the meters annoyed automobile drivers, they were a financial success. Meters were soon being used in cities throughout the country. Twenty-five years after the first meter was installed, it was estimated that Americans had put an average of fifty million coins per year into parking _____ .

>   meters   taxes   parkings

This passage is about the invention of the

(a) parking garage.
(b) automobile.
(c) parking meter.
(d) parking lot.

60 | Some of the world's best-known pieces of art have strange histories. For instance, in 1660 a prominent British citizen commissioned a statue to commemorate the return of King Charles II to England after his long exile from the country. The chosen sculptor just happened to have on hand an appropriate statue for the occasion. The statue was of the current Polish king, riding on horseback over the body of a defeated Turkish soldier. It had been rejected by the monarch. So the sculptor decided to remodel the statue for the English king's monument. He altered the faces and dress of the two men, creating an image of Charles II riding over the body of his vanquished enemy, Oliver Cromwell. The statue was acclaimed as a great work of art, although the sculptor had forgotten one detail: he had left a Turkish turban on the head of the conquered _____ .

>   **Charles   king   Cromwell**

This passage is about

(a) popular art in seventeenth-century England.
(b) reasons for the exile of Charles II.
(c) a short history of the Polish-Turkish war.
(d) an artistic mix-up with a humorous consequence.

61 | Who would better symbolize the importance of working to prevent forest fires than the lone survivor of a devastating fire? Smokey the Bear was a real bear. He was raised in a zoo after his mother was killed in a forest fire in 1950, when he was still a cub. Most bears don't like living in captivity, but Smokey thrived in the zoo and soon became a favorite with the visitors and staff. Wildlife and conservation magazines started to use pictures of him to promote forest fire prevention, and Smokey quickly became a national symbol for fire safety. He became so famous that Congress passed a law forbidding the use of his name for any other _____.

bear   forest   fire

This passage is about

(a) forest fires.
(b) conservation magazines.
(c) Smokey the Bear.
(d) a terrible forest fire in 1950.

62 | On Thursday December 1, 1955, a tired seamstress named Rosa Parks was asked to give up her seat on a bus to a white man and move to the back of a Montgomery, Alabama, bus. The forty-two-year-old black woman quietly refused and was subsequently arrested. Her arrest sparked a 381-day bus boycott that helped launch the civil rights movement in the United States and the career of civil rights leader Martin Luther King, Jr. Both Rosa Parks's arrest and the bus boycott became vehicles for drawing attention to the rights of blacks. When Rosa Parks was convicted, her case was appealed to the United States Supreme Court, which ruled that discrimination on buses was a violation of federal law. The bus boycott was also a success, for the bus company went bankrupt without its black passengers. The simple protest of one woman helped to win equal rights for millions of people throughout the

_____.

country   state   rights

This passage is about

(a) civil rights leaders of the South.
(b) the life of Rosa Parks.
(c) Supreme Court rulings on racial discrimination.
(d) the incident that began the civil rights movement.

63 | Did George Washington really chop down a cherry tree? This children's story is intended as a lesson in honesty, because young Washington bravely admits to his father that he chopped the tree down. Whether or not this is true, people in the United States use the story as an excuse to eat cherry pie on any patriotic occasion, sometimes quite a bit of it. In the town of George, Washington, the 273 citizens bake themselves a twelve-hundred-pound cherry pie every Independence Day. But the world's record for cherry pie baking was set in 1976, in honor of the United States' bicentennial. In Charlevoix, Michigan, a seven-ton pie was baked, using two and a half tons of _____ .

books   cherries   people

A good title for this passage might be

(a) A Slice of Americana.
(b) George Washington's Favorite Pie.
(c) Small Town Blues.
(d) The Bicentennial.

64 | Congressman Hiram Johnson wanted to be president of the United States, not vice president, so he refused to take the secondary slot that would have helped him achieve his ambition. Republican party leaders thought that Johnson would make a good running mate for Henry Knox in the 1920 election. They told Johnson that Knox was in poor health, so it was likely that Johnson would eventually be called upon to serve as president if Knox was elected. Johnson refused, however, saying, "You would put a heartbeat between me and the White House? Never!" Later, when Warren Harding was chosen instead of Knox to be the Republican party's candidate, Johnson was again asked if he would like to be vice president, and he again refused. Harding did not live to serve his full term, so Johnson's refusal cost him the _____ .

election   party   presidency

This passage is about

(a) death and the American presidency.
(b) the pride that cost Hiram Johnson the presidency.
(c) the duties of a United States vice president.
(d) the presidency of Warren Harding.

65 The Javanese and the Malayans found an unusual way to avoid a war 1,500 years ago. The two southeast Asian countries disagreed about who owned the island of Sumatra, so they held a bullfight to decide the issue. The general of each army picked a strong bull. Then the bulls fought each other in a huge arena while thousands of spectators from Java and Malaya watched. After a long and bloody struggle, the Malayan bull killed the Javanese bull. Both countries accepted the outcome of the bullfight as the final decision on Sumatra's ownership. Malaya won the island of Sumatra from Java without shedding the blood of a single _____.

soldier   bull   island

This passage is about

(a) a bullfight that prevented a war.
(b) how to win a bullfight.
(c) sports in southeast Asia.
(d) island countries in Asia.

66 King Richard the Lionhearted got his nickname for being a brave warrior and a progressive military scientist, not a conscientious ruler. In fact, King Richard I spent most of his ten-year reign on a crusade into Palestine. He was in England for only six months of those ten years. Richard was known for doing anything necessary to win a battle. He spent two years striving to take the port of Acre, the most strategically important city in the Holy Land. It is said that Richard finally won the battle, in the year 1192, with an imaginative trick. He had his soldiers throw one hundred beehives over the walls of the city. The enraged insects so mangled the defenders of Acre that they surrendered unconditionally. Richard took the city, but he probably waited until the bees were _____.

gone   old   calm

This passage is about

(a) the life of King Richard I.
(b) King Richard the Lionhearted's unusual battle strategy.
(c) the crusades in the Holy Land.
(d) unusual uses for bees.

67 | Many Americans are not aware of the fact that John Wilkes Booth wasn't the first man to take a shot at President Abraham Lincoln. In fact, before that fatal night at Ford's Theater, there had been two other assassination attempts. In 1861, Lincoln was riding alone to visit a veterans hospital called Soldier's Home when a man took a few shots at him from fifty yards away. In August of 1864, also on the road to Soldier's Home, an unknown gunman started shooting at Lincoln, missing him by just a few inches. The bullets went right through the top of Lincoln's stovepipe hat. Lincoln insisted on taking these incidents in stride, and ordered that they not be _____.

remembered   forgotten   publicized

This passage deals with

(a) two little-known attempts on President Lincoln's life.
(b) firearms in the nineteenth century.
(c) Lincoln's interest in Soldier's Home.
(d) Lincoln's unusual sense of modesty.

68 | Moviegoers all over the world fell in love with Mary Pickford, "America's Sweetheart." Pickford appeared in hundreds of films and became a major star during the era of silent films. Many of her roles were in the landmark films of D.W. Griffith, who was a great director of both silent and sound pictures. Mary Pickford often played young girls, and she became a symbol for innocent American girlhood. But Pickford's image was more romantic than realistic. She was actually a talented actress and businesswoman, not an innocent little girl. With her husband, Douglas Fairbanks, and Charlie Chaplin, two other silent film superstars, she founded United Artists Films. And many people never realized that America's sweetheart was not a native American, but that she actually came from _____.

Canada   Connecticut   Colorado

This passage is about the

(a) founding of United Artists Films.
(b) rise and fall of silent movies.
(c) career of Mary Pickford.
(d) silent film era.

69 | What does a tire company know about restaurants and culinary excellence? Michelin, a French rubber firm, now publishes the most prestigious restaurant guide in the world. To rate the restaurants, it uses a star system, with one star meaning good, two, excellent, and three, world-class. Recently, the Michelin guide surveyed 3,036 French restaurants, with the following results: 2,384 received no star, 581 were awarded one star, 62 received two stars, and just 11 received three stars. Five of these 11 world-class restaurants are located in Paris. Those who agree with the results, then, would say that it's true—a rubber company can have the last word in _____.

rubber   food   tires

This passage is about

(a) bad restaurants in Paris, France.
(b) a rubber company that publishes a restaurant guide.
(c) various ways to prepare and eat rubber.
(d) the best restaurants in the world.

70 | Ignatius Trebitsch was born into a Jewish Hungarian family in 1889, but he belonged to five other faiths before the end of his life. At the age of eighteen he moved to Germany and was baptized into the Lutheran church. Later, during a sojourn in England, he became a Quaker and a member of Parliament before switching over to the Anglican faith and becoming a spy for the Germans. Trebitsch's next stop was North America, where he turned up as a Presbyterian minister in Canada. When World War I broke out, Trebitsch returned to Germany and then shipped out to India, where he was accepted into a Buddhist monastery. High in the mountains of the subcontinent, the Hungarian found a home: he lived the last seventeen years of his life as a disciple of _____.

Muhammad   Moses   Buddha

This passage is about

(a) a man who experienced many religions.
(b) the greatest spy in the world.
(c) how all the world's religions are related.
(d) Jewish Presbyterians in Hungary.

71 | First impressions can be important, and they can also be misleading. A perfect example is the meeting that took place in 1645 between Czar Alexis of Russia and his prospective bride. The lady, Eudoxia, was beautiful and aristocratic, and she was considered a perfect match for the monarch of the Russian empire. For their first meeting she was clothed in an impressive gown and precious jewels, and her hair was carefully braided. Unfortunately, it was braided too tightly; Eudoxia's hairstyle hurt her so much that she fainted as she bowed to the Czar. Not knowing why she had fainted, he decided that she must be an epileptic, so he called off the _____.

funeral   engagement   empire

This passage is about

(a) the reign of the Russian Czar Alexis.
(b) the marriage customs of Russian royalty.
(c) fashions in seventeenth-century Russia.
(d) the misleading first impression Czar Alexis got of Eudoxia.

72 | Watching television won't ruin your eyes, reading a lot won't cause you to need glasses, and reading in dim light doesn't damage eyes. For centuries, doctors advised people to avoid straining their eyes, but modern science has shown that the eyes are tougher than doctors long thought. The Greek physician Paul of Aegina was one of the first doctors to advise against reading more than a few hours a day. A Persian doctor named Rhazes gave patients similar advice in the tenth century, when he told them to avoid books with small print. Twentieth-century doctor Edward S. Gifford contradicts those ancient medical opinions, saying that there is no such thing as eyestrain: people can use their eyes in the most difficult circumstances without permanent _____.

damage   glasses   contacts

This passage is about

(a) the structure of the human eyeball.
(b) the best conditions in which to read.
(c) the modern discovery that strain doesn't damage eyes.
(d) modern treatments for vision problems.

73 | The legend of Romulus and Remus is probably the most famous story about human children raised by a wolf, but in 1920, there appeared another wolf-child story. Supposedly, a missionary in India was asked by the natives to help rid their village of two "man-ghosts." The missionary agreed to help and carefully watched the area where the ghosts had reportedly been seen. That evening, to his astonishment, he saw two human shapes crawl from a hole in the ground. During daylight, he dug up the area and exposed an underground den containing two children and several wolf cubs. Unfortunately, the girls died soon after they were discovered, without learning to speak or walk. The missionary who found them never learned how the two children had come to be raised by a _____.

wolf   bear   fox

This passage is about

(a) the work of missionaries in India.
(b) two children raised by a wolf.
(c) the legend of Romulus and Remus.
(d) village life in India.

74 | A bowie knife is a long, stout hunting knife with a blade that is ten to fifteen inches long and two inches wide. It was originally carried by hunters in the western and southwestern parts of the United States. Knife experts disagree about the origin of the knife's name. According to one story, it is named after Colonel Jim Bowie, a notorious character from Lagna County, Kentucky. Bowie was a friend of the famous western explorers Davy Crockett and William B. Davis, both of whom were killed with Bowie at the battle of the Alamo in 1836. Other authorities say that the first bowie knife was made by R.P. Bowie in about 1820. Although the blade of that knife was smaller, about nine and a half inches long and one and a half inches wide, it was also made for _____.

whittling   eating   hunting

This passage is about

(a) the siege of the Alamo.
(b) Jim Bowie.
(c) the origin of the name of the bowie knife.
(d) the rise of the R.P. Bowie Company.

75 | While many people are unnecessarily terrified of all snakes, a cautious respect for some snakes is well warranted. The venom of many snakes is highly poisonous. In fact, a snake's venom is often harmful to all living things—plants as well as animals and humans. In some cases, it is even fatal to the snake itself. There have been instances in which rattlesnakes, after being irritated and annoyed in their cages, have moved suddenly and accidentally struck their own bodies with their fangs. Soon afterward, the snakes rolled over and died. Contrary to what you might expect, the venom, which is secreted directly from the blood of the snake, will poison the snake if it is reintroduced into the reptile's own

_____ .

venom   poison   bloodstream

This passage deals mainly with

(a) the venom of snakes.
(b) antidotes to snake venom.
(c) how to recognize a poisonous snake.
(d) why people fear snakes.

76 | Some insects can be quite cunning, using the resources of their environments to help them survive. The assassin bug, a natural enemy of termites, is a good example. It uses a bodily secretion similar to glue to paste pieces of a termite nest onto itself, and then it hides near the entrance of the nest. Termites leaving the nest do not notice the assassin, because it is disguised as a part of the nest. The termites are easy prey for the assassin, which catches and disembowels a termite and then uses the empty body to lure other termites out of the nest. A single assassin will use this method to catch up to thirty termites for a single meal. Dr. Elizabeth McMahon of the University of North Carolina sees this as an example of an insect using tools, demonstrating that the assassin bug is _____ .

stupid   clumsy   intelligent

This passage is about

(a) termites.
(b) assassin termites.
(c) the assassin bug.
(d) killer insects.

77 | Most people today buy bread instead of making their own, but this is a recent development in the history of bread-making. Although New York City and other towns had had bakeries for many years, in the early 1900s, 95 percent of all bread in the United States was still baked at home. By the 1950s, about 95 percent of American bread was baked commercially. The change in bread-baking habits was influenced by industrialization. Baking just a few loaves of bread at home takes a lot of time, but large modern bakeries can turn out as many as thirteen thousand loaves per hour. That means that a bread factory can bake as much bread in half an hour as a nineteenth-century homemaker baked in her entire _____.

life   country   oven

This passage is about

(a) the change in bread-baking and buying habits.
(b) how bread is mass-produced.
(c) the nutritional value of bakery bread.
(d) why people like to bake bread.

78 | In his ode to the American flag, "The Star Spangled Banner," Francis Scott Key wrote of the British rockets giving off a "red glare." The rockets used in the Revolutionary War were the deadly invention of British firemaster Sir William Congreve, and they were designed to destroy the American forces. Those early rockets were simple tubes stuffed with gunpowder, topped with an iron warhead, and guided by preset rudders. After a flight of about two miles, Congreve's rockets would shatter into thousands of pieces of searing shrapnel. Impressive as those first rockets used on the North American continent were, the British failed to capture Fort McHenry, and they eventually lost the _____.

cause   poem   war

This passage is about

(a) the rockets used by the British in the American Revolutionary War.
(b) how the British won the Revolutionary War.
(c) Francis Scott Key's poem "The Star Spangled Banner."
(d) British firemaster Sir William Congreve.

79 | Jean Paul Marat was one of the most radical leaders of the French Revolution. With Danton and Robespierre, Marat was responsible for the murderous Reign of Terror. Marat was a doctor at the start of the revolution. He published a newspaper calling for the death of people he claimed were anti-revolutionary. Mobs stirred up by his writings carried out the September Massacre of 1792, in which more than 1,000 people were killed. Marat's writings were so violent that he was tried for sedition, or causing rebellion, in 1793. But he was freed. A young woman named Charlotte Corday, who believed that Marat must be killed to save France from more violent riots, stabbed him to death in his bath later that year. It was a violent end for a violent _____.

woman   paper   man

This passage is about

(a) the history of the French Revolution.
(b) mobs during the Reign of Terror.
(c) the radical revolutionary leader Jean Paul Marat.
(d) the life of Charlotte Corday.

80 | When the prophet Muhammed brought the word of Allah to the peoples of the Middle East, it was the beginning of a story that would soon affect half the world. The year of Muhammed's death, A.D. 632, saw Islam begin an expansion from a tiny corner of Arabia to the very gates of Europe and China. By 750, Muslims had carried their swords and their religion to Persia, Egypt, Syria, India, Central Asia, North Africa and Spain. As they conquered new territories, they gave their captives a simple but harsh choice. They could convert to the religion of Islam or they could die. Soon, one third of the world's population had become Muslim. The Muslims continued their wave of conquest until the bloody battle of Tours, France, in 732, in which they were _____.

defeated   converted   persuaded

This passage is about

(a) the life of the Islamic prophet Muhammed.
(b) the defeat of the Islamic empire.
(c) how the early Christians conquered the world.
(d) the early history of the Muslims.

81 | In a battle, the weaker opponent can sometimes win by being clever and using the enemy's own weapons against them. This was demonstrated by the U.S.S. *Eagle* during the War of 1812. The *Eagle* fought the heavily armed British ship H.M.S. *Dispatch* in a battle that began off the coast of Long Island, New York. The *Dispatch* nearly sank the *Eagle*, but the American sailors managed to get to a nearby beach, where they dragged their guns onto the sand dunes and waited for the British to start firing at them. After each cannonball was fired from the *Dispatch*, the Americans retrieved it and fired it back. This odd sort of fighting continued for several hours before the British finally retreated. The Americans had won the _____.

ship   cannon   battle

This passage is about

(a) how the British won the War of 1812.
(b) how the Americans manufactured ammunition.
(c) how to fire used cannonballs.
(d) an odd naval battle in the War of 1812.

82 | Zoning is a way of controlling land use by regulating the kinds of buildings that can be built in certain areas. Zoning is mainly used in urban areas. It is used together with other city-planning techniques to control the physical and business layout of a city or town. Zoning was first used in European cities in the late nineteenth century. German and Swedish cities used zoning when new land was being developed to be part of the cities. Zoning controlled the heights and number of buildings and helped avoid overcrowding. Zoning in the United States has been mainly concerned with the function, rather than the size, of buildings. In the U.S., the locations of stores, businesses and industry are all controlled by _____.

business   zoning   industry

This passage is mainly about

(a) the meaning and uses of zoning.
(b) nineteenth-century German cities.
(c) business and industry in the U.S.
(d) various city-planning techniques.

54

83 | In medieval times, there were few opportunities for women to improve their positions in life, but a British girl named Bathilde is one who got lucky. Her luck began, however, with a piece of misfortune. Bathilde was captured by seafaring pirates and sold into slavery in France. Her life was not happy, until she was acquired by the court of King Clovis II of France. As Bathilde matured into a beautiful woman, the king himself took notice, and Bathilde won Clovis's heart and was married to him before she was twenty-five years old. After the king died, Bathilde became ruler of France, and she decreed an end to slavery in that country. In just a few years, Bathilde had risen from slave girl to wise

_____ .

monarch   housewife   man

Which would be the best title for this passage?

(a) Queen for a Day
(b) Career Search
(c) War Is Over
(d) Rags to Riches

84 | Animals have spent more time in space than humans have. Since the United States and the Soviet Union began sending rockets and satellites into space, dogs, spiders, bees, guppies, and chimps have all become astronauts. Some of them tested the conditions of space flight before human astronauts were sent into space—the Soviets sent dogs, and the United States used chimps in early flights. Other animals have been used for scientific experiments to find out how living creatures react to various conditions in space. Spiders have spun webs inside spacecraft cabins. Ant colonies have made the trip into space in glass terrariums. Animals have made great contributions to space _____ .

travel   animals   conditions

This passage is mostly about

(a) animals used in space travel.
(b) spaceships built for animals.
(c) Soviet space technology.
(d) early space travel.

85 | Though visitors to zoos are usually allowed to get quite close to llamas and camels, it's wise to avoid getting too close. It's not that these animals are dangerous, it's just that they have what to most of us would seem to be a bad habit: they spit. And their saliva smells strong and vile. Llamas and camels developed this trait both to protect themselves from other animals and to show their annoyance with other llamas and camels (or sometimes, as in zoos, with human beings). It would seem to be smartest to view these creatures from a safe _____ .

distance　　　zoo　　　habit

This passage is about

(a) the fact that camels and llamas spit.
(b) how llamas and camels are treated in zoos.
(c) why people shouldn't tease llamas.
(d) how animals protect themselves.

86 | Ever since the thirteenth century, there has been a London Bridge crossing the Thames River in London, but it has not always been the same bridge. The first London Bridge, built in 1209, lasted 623 years. It saw the bubonic plague come and go, survived the Great London Fire of 1666, and suffered alternating stages of neglect and renovation, until a new bridge was finally built in 1832. That London Bridge is the one that now stands in Lake Havasu City, Arizona. In 1967, the bridge was taken apart in London, shipped, and rebuilt, stone by stone, in its new location. Why did the original London Bridge last more than six hundred years and the second one only sixty-five? The nineteenth-century bridge builders simply couldn't foresee the invention of the automobile. By 1967, London Bridge just couldn't handle the traffic. The newest London Bridge, opened in 1973, is one of fifteen bridges now spanning the Thames, and can handle plenty of cars with its six traffic _____ .

police　　　lights　　　lanes

The subject of this passage is

(a) rivers in London.
(b) tourism in Lake Havasu City, Arizona.
(c) the effect of the automobile on bridges.
(d) the three London Bridges.

87 | Germ warfare has been highly developed in the twentieth century, but armies have been killing enemies with disease since ancient times. The Romans and the Germanic tribes that conquered them would hurl dead bodies into cities under siege. This demoralized the people trapped in the cities, and the rotting flesh spread disease. In medieval times, soldiers launched dead horses over the walls of fortresses. At the siege of Carolstein in 1422, the townspeople were pelted with two hundred wagon loads of cow manure. Germ warfare has existed throughout history; in this century it has merely been carried to new _____.

fighting   extremes   death

This passage is about

(a) modern warfare.
(b) the horror of war in medieval times.
(c) germ warfare throughout history.
(d) modern germ warfare.

88 | General Nathanael Greene's most famous victory in the American Revolution was gained when he lost a battle. Greene was in charge of the American armies in North and South Carolina, where British General Cornwallis was hoping for a major victory. Rather than confronting the British troops, which outnumbered his, Greene retreated, forcing the British to follow him deeper into the wilderness. After being joined by reinforcements, Greene turned and fought. But the British won, so Greene and his troops moved still farther inland. Though the British won the battle, they suffered the loss of a quarter of their men. The rest were near starvation and out of ammunition, and they were far from their supply depots. Soon Cornwallis had to turn back toward the coast. The British general's retreat allowed the Americans to build up their forces, and the British never got so far into the Carolinas

_____.

again   soon   before

The subject of this passage is

(a) famous British generals in the American Revolution.
(b) the British victory at Guilford Courthouse.
(c) the end of the American Revolution.
(d) General Greene's clever defeat of the British troops.

89 | Malaria is a tropical illness most commonly found in the forest regions of Central and South America, central Africa and parts of southern Asia. It is spread by a species of mosquito that breeds in the warm, swampy pools found in those parts of the world. The symptoms of malaria are high fever, chills and weakness. In India, almost a million people die each year from the disease. In the sixteenth century, scientists discovered that it could be controlled with quinine, a drug made from the bark of the cinchona tree. In modern times, spraying the mosquitoes' breeding grounds has greatly reduced the risk of _____ .

malaria   fever   death

The subject of this passage is

(a) malaria.
(b) mosquitoes.
(c) quinine.
(d) Indians.

90 | Alchemy (AL-kuh-mee) is a blend of science, magic and religion that was popular from the time of early Christians until about 1700. Alchemists tried to find a method for turning lesser metals into silver and gold, and they also searched for an elixir of life that would cure disease and lengthen life. Although some alchemists were fakes, others were learned men who felt that if they could make gold from lesser metals they could also learn how to perfect other things. Some alchemy was practiced in China and India before the birth of Christ, but it developed more strongly in Egypt during the following three hundred years. It spread to the Arabs in Syria and Persia, and finally reached western Europe in the twelfth and thirteenth centuries. People believed that gold's ability to remain unchanged over time—to maintain its quality—could be transferred to other objects and to people, so that the techniques used to make gold could get rid of physical corruption and _____ .

gold   silver   death

This passage is about

(a) magicians in the Egyptian empire.
(b) metal mining in ancient Persia.
(c) the meaning and history of alchemy.
(d) how to turn lesser metals into silver and gold.

91 | One of the most mischievous practical jokers in the United States was a man named Hugh Troy. Troy started playing practical jokes on people while he was a student at Cornell University. One day he discovered a wastepaper basket that had been made from the foot of a rhinoceros. Unable to resist the opportunity for a joke, Troy took the foot and used it to make tracks across the campus and onto a frozen reservoir. The tracks ended at the edge of a large hole in the ice. Zoologists confirmed the authenticity of the tracks, and many people in the community complained that their drinking water tasted of rhinoceros. After finishing school, Troy went into the army where he had a desk job. To protest the volume of unnecessary paperwork, he created a report that recorded the number of flies caught each day on the flypaper hung in the mess hall. He sent the report to the Pentagon, and soon the Pentagon required every unit to send in a flypaper _____.

student   joke   report

This passage is about

(a) flypaper reports.
(b) rhinoceros tracks.
(c) a practical joker.
(d) Cornell University.

92 | Smoke detectors in the home can save lives, but to be most effective they should be installed in the places where fires are most likely to occur. The United States National Fire Protection Agency says that smoke alarms should be placed on every floor of the house, including the attic and basement, where fires can start in crowded storage areas. Hallways near communal rooms and stairways are other good locations for smoke detectors. Don't place them in the kitchen, near a fireplace, or in the garage, however, for the alarm may be triggered by smoke or steam that is normally produced in those _____.

fires   areas   containers

This passage is about

(a) where smoke detectors should be installed.
(b) how a smoke detector works.
(c) how to respond to a fire alarm.
(d) various types of smoke detectors.

93 | Many professional athletes are able to play a variety of sports well. For example, basketball star Dave DeBuschere also played major league baseball with the Chicago White Sox. Jackie Robinson was an all-American college football player before he became the first black man to play major league baseball. But no player has excelled in more sports than Lionel "Big Train" Conacher, who played in the National Hockey League. Conacher's family couldn't afford to buy him ice skates until he was sixteen, but just six years later he was playing professional hockey. He also played baseball for a Toronto team of the Triple-A International League. Baseball great Ty Cobb once said that Conacher had the talent to play in the major leagues. Conacher also held the light-heavyweight boxing title in Canada, played for a professional football team, and was a fine lacrosse player. It seems that Lionel Conacher really was what people sometimes call a natural _____.

athlete   player   sport

This passage is about

(a) a versatile athlete.
(b) major baseball leagues.
(c) the life of Jackie Robinson.
(d) professional football.

94 | At the beginning of the twentieth century, there were no such things as rockets or even airplanes, but Americans were certainly already obsessed with things that traveled fast. In 1905, the Pennsylvania Railroad introduced what was then the fastest train in the world; it made the trip from New York to Chicago in eighteen hours. Then, the New York Central Railroad laid its own line, and its train also made the trip in eighteen hours. These early attempts at high-speed rail travel, however, sacrificed safety for speed. Within a week of their first runs, both trains suffered fatal _____.

bankruptcy   wrecks   criticism

This passage focuses on

(a) the American obsession with speed in the twentieth century.
(b) the fate of two early high-speed railway lines.
(c) the invention of the airplane.
(d) the founding of the Pennsylvania Railroad.

95 | In orbit around the Earth are 3,173 objects that are parts from rockets and satellites that were sent into space. Three-quarters of the vehicle junk comes from satellites sent up by the United States and the Soviet Union. The space trash includes spent rocket stages, bolts, tether cables, separation springs, de-spin weights and other fragments. Forty-six other pieces of satellite junk have escaped Earth's orbit and gone off into outer space, while more than four thousand pieces have fallen back to Earth or burned up in the atmosphere. Many of the celestial objects that streak through the night sky on their way to Earth are simply returning to the place where they were _____ .

made   burned   destroyed

This passage is about

(a) space junk.
(b) satellites in space.
(c) deep space trash collecting procedures.
(d) the international space race.

96 | Early people thought that serious and disabling diseases were caused by demons or angry gods. They believed that a spirit either put something such as a dart, stone or worm into the body of the victim, or invaded the victim's body and forced out his or her soul. Treatments included suction, which was sometimes used to try to remove an object that was believed to have been put inside the person, and incantations, which were used to persuade evil spirits to leave. One method used for making an escape route for a disease was boring a hole in the victim's skull—the practice of trepanning (trih-PAN-ing). Prehistoric trepanned skulls have been found in Europe and Peru. It is the oldest known surgical operation, and the practice still exists among some primitive peoples, but it has mostly died _____ .

over   in   out

This passage is about

(a) why people no longer believe that disease is caused by spirits.
(b) ancient beliefs about diseases.
(c) how to perform a trepanning operation.
(d) why prehistoric trepanned skulls were found in Europe.

97 | An icebreaker is an enormous vessel that plunges through thick ocean ice, opening paths for other ships and boats. Icebreakers also rescue ships that have become caught in ice. They use their strongly reinforced hulls and great engine power to demolish thin or brittle ice. To break thick ice, they employ their enormous weight by driving their bow ends up on top of the ice; ice that is several feet thick will give way under the bow of a heavy icebreaker. Some icebreakers run on atomic power. The nuclear-powered Soviet ship *Lenin*, which is the world's largest and heaviest icebreaker, is one of these. The ship, which weighs 16,000 tons, began breaking ice in 1960 along the coast of the Soviet _____.

States   ships   Union

This passage is about

(a) nuclear-powered ships.
(b) icebound ships.
(c) the Soviet ship *Lenin*.
(d) ships called icebreakers.

98 | The largest Christian church in the world is Saint Peter's Church in Vatican City. Also called Saint Peter's Basilica, it is the second church to stand above the crypt, or tomb, that is believed to hold the body of Saint Peter, the first pope of the Roman Catholic Church. Saint Peter's is built in the shape of a cross, 700 feet long and about 450 feet at its widest point. The nave, or center aisle, is 150 feet high, and a magnificent dome rises more than 400 feet from the floor of the church and measures 138 feet in diameter. The church was built over a period of 150 years by ten different architects, including two famous Baroque sculptors, Giovanni Lorenzo Bernini and Michelangelo. Decorated with marble, gilding, mosaics and sculpture, the church contains some of the most precious works of art in the _____.

church   building   world

This passage is about

(a) the original church built over Saint Peter's crypt.
(b) Saint Peter's Church, in Rome.
(c) the art works of Michelangelo.
(d) historic cathedrals in Italy.

99 | The escalator was invented in the United States, but the first department store to install one was Harrods, in London, England. Jesse W. Reno patented his Reno Inclined Elevator in March 1892. It was an inclined conveyor belt made up of wooden slats joined with rubber cleats. An electric motor moved the belt at a speed of one and a half miles per hour. Harrods installed its Reno Inclined Elevator in 1898 and had a porter stand at the top, ready to serve brandy to any passengers who felt faint after their ride. Inventors Charles A. Wheeler and Charles D. Seaberger later improved the design by adding flat steps to the conveyor, creating a moving staircase. It was at the Paris Exposition of 1900 that the invention finally received the name by which it is known today, the _____ .

elevator   staircase   escalator

This passage is about the

(a) invention of the elevator.
(b) invention of the escalator.
(c) first English department store.
(d) Paris Exposition of 1900.

100 | Cats ran wild for many thousands of years after dogs had become pets and servants to humans. The Egyptians tamed the first cats about four thousand years ago. They associated those small, lean African wild cats with the Egyptian cat-headed goddess, Bast, but the cats were working deities. They were highly valued because they killed rodents that attacked Egyptian food stores and granaries, eating food and spreading sickness. They were such an important defense against famine and disease that killing a cat, even by accident, was a crime punishable by death. Although it was illegal to export Egyptian cats, cats had been smuggled to all parts of Europe by 900 B.C. Since then, many different varieties of cats have been bred, and they are popular pets all over the _____ .

country   island   world

This passage is about

(a) dogs in ancient Egypt.
(b) Egyptian granaries.
(c) cat goddesses in Egypt.
(d) the domestication of cats.